Kiss of Life

A Coloring Book to Celebrate Life & Adoption

by April McCallum

ISBN: 978-1-7325752-0-2

Kiss of Life: A Coloring Book to Celebrate Life & Adoption
(c) 2019 by April McCallum
Published in the United States by Heart & Key Publishing

Cover Design Collaboration and Colorization by Pete Berg
www.aprilmccallumdesigns.com

All rights reserved.
No part of this book may be reproduced or transmitted by any form or by any means, electronic or mechanical including photocopy recording, or any information storage or retrieval system, without prior written consent from the author.

Welcome!

Art and Heart... I'm so happy you found your way here. This collection of coloring pages was created with love, just for you. A powerful combination of beautiful hand-drawn art and quotes to celebrate and honor the heart of adoption.

Each one of my coloring books for adults has special meaning to me, but especially, *Kiss of Life*. Most people have a personal connection to adoption, their own story or someone they know, and I am no exception.

Kiss of Life was designed to be a thoughtful and beautiful celebration of adoption, the love of mothers — *birth and adoptive mothers* — families, and the treasure they share in common. Adoption is a bittersweet gift. Bitter because it's an agonizing rending of the heart. The heart of the one who loved, protected and carried a treasured piece of herself in her womb. Sweet because it is not a giving up, rather, the careful placement of this greatly beloved treasure, this child and its destiny, into the hands and heart of another for safekeeping. The heart of one who will carry it with magnificent love the rest of the journey.

> *"Little One, May my love give you strength for your journey, grace for your troubles, confidence for your dreams, joy for your dance, music for your song, light for your path, wisdom for your road, wings for your spirit, rainbows for your soul and fullness for your heart."* — April McCallum

Tips: If you would like to practice your lines and coloring tools, you will find a blank page in the back of the book to do just that. If you plan to use non-dry coloring materials, please place a blank sheet under the page you're coloring so it doesn't bleed through. Consider this book a place for you to feel gratitude expressed through your mindful and joy-filled coloring experience.

To life and love and the power of adoption!

XO
April

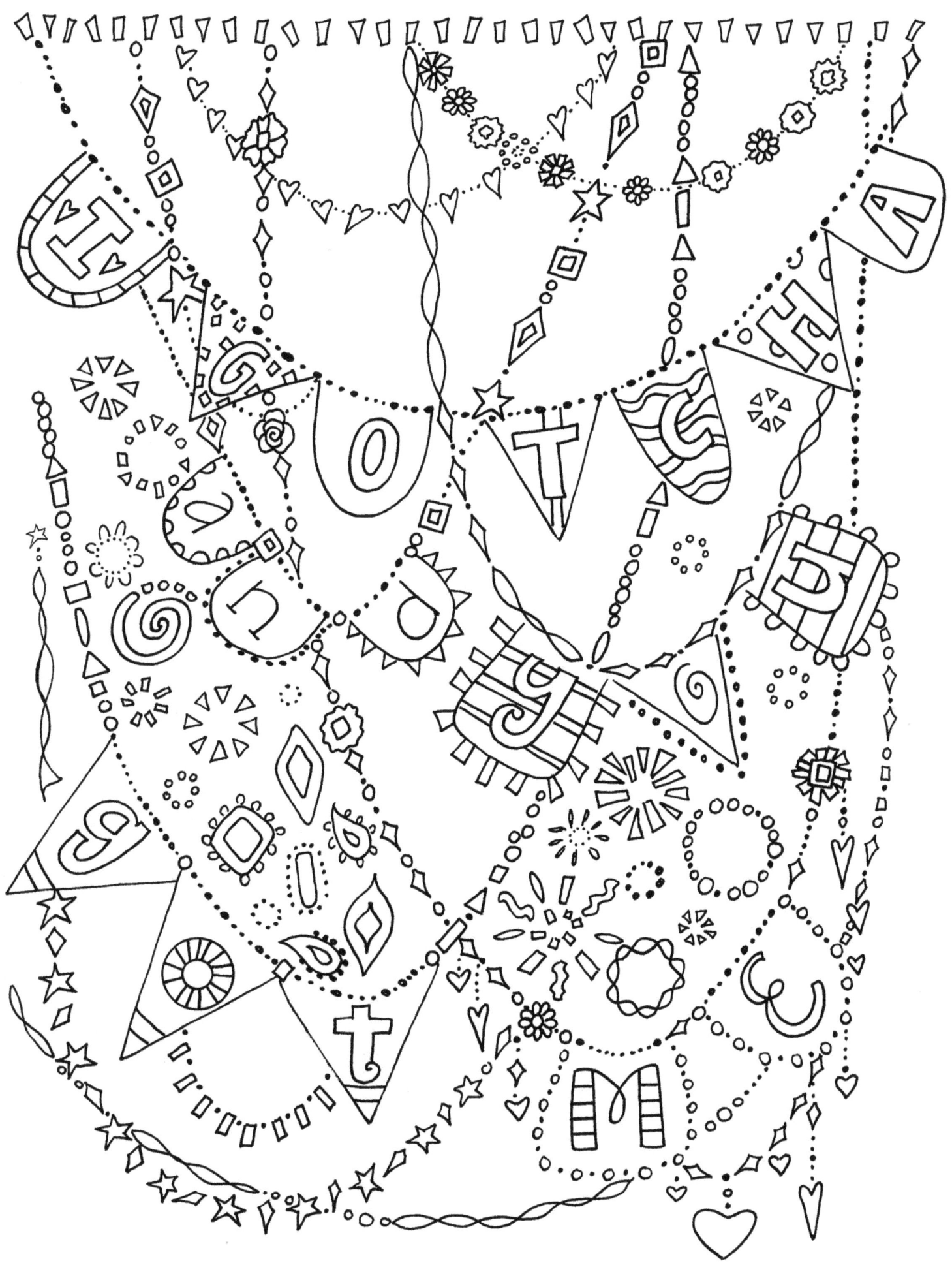

my sweet little one

You were *handmade* with LOVE with a plan & a special purpose to love and be loved in this crazy world. May you be brave and strong, Bold in truth, kind and COURAGEOUS, Generous in spirit, unafraid, a dreamer and conqueror of big dreams. FILLED with JOY and laughter & every good thing. always remember YOU are LOVED

i love you because the entire universe conspired to help me find ♥ YOU

— P. Coelho

"I know the plans I have for you,
plans to prosper you and not harm you,
plans to give you hope and a future."
– *Book of Jeremiah*

"Home should be an anchor,
a port in a storm, a refuge,
a happy place in which to dwell,
a place where we are loved
and where we can love."
– *M. J. Ashton*

A Little About April...

April McCallum is an illustrator, cartoonist and writer.
Since retiring from a successful career in the high-tech industry, she's focused her creative passions on art, writing and advocacy projects. Her artwork has been licensed and featured on magazine covers, for business and non-profits, and on a variety of gift products. Her writing and artwork has appeared in a variety of magazines and featured on CNBC. Her signature style combines words and visuals, color and design. Her writing and illustration work is inspirational, hope-filled and empowering, while her cartoonist side brings a unique twist of humor to the table.

April has long been an advocacy artist designing creative pieces that interweave words and visuals to speak to issues close to her heart. Current topics include empowering women, adoption, breast cancer awareness, grief and loss, addiction and the power of one.

COLORS OF HOPE: Breast Cancer Warriors Coloring Book
REFLECTIONS OF LOVE: Coloring Book Therapy for Grief & Loss
BRAVE WINGS: A Coloring Book to Celebrate & Empower Women
KISS OF LIFE: A Coloring Book to Celebrate Life & Adoption

Pete Berg and April McCallum have been creative collaborators on a variety of colorful and interesting projects over the years. If you would like to connect with Pete Berg regarding a graphic art project, he can be reached at: ohberg3@gmail.com

Website: www.aprilmccallumdesigns.com
Email: april@aprilmccallumdesigns.com
Blog: DestinysWomen.com
Facebook: @AprilMcCallumDesigns
Instagram: @AprilCartoons | @AprilLovesColor | @PinkCartoons
Pinterest: https://www.pinterest.com/aprilmccallum/

To my beautiful Anne-Marie
whose unconditional love helped give me comfort to dance and sing
whose jeweled heart gave me the peace to lift my wings

www.ingramcontent.com/pod-product-compliance
Lightning Source LLC
Chambersburg PA
CBHW081015040426
42444CB00014B/3225